AF541040

www.ingramcontent.com/pod-product-compliance
Lightning Source LLC
Chambersburg PA
CBHW042043160726
48282CB00038B/1266

* 9 7 8 8 1 1 9 9 4 6 3 3 4 *

Al Qaida Al Nooraniya

الشيخ نور محمد حقاني

Shaykh Noor Muhammad Haqqani

بِسْمِ اللّٰهِ الرَّحْمٰنِ الرَّحِيْمِ

Lesson No. 1 The Alphabets

Instructions

The alphabet is the foundation of reading and writing, so it deserves special focus. Pay attention to children's pronunciation and recognizing sounds associated with each letter. Guide them to read from left to right, top to bottom and in reverse, and differentiate between bold and light letters. Consistent practice ensures a strong foundation, which benefits both students and teachers in the long run.

حا ح Haa	جيم ج Jeem	ثا ث Thaa	تا ت Taa	با ب Baa	ألف ا Alif
سين س Seen	زا ز Zaa	را ر Raa	ذال ذ Zaal	دال د Daal	خا خ Khaa
عين ع Aeen	ظا ظ Zuaa	طا ط Tuaa	ضاد ض Duaad	صاد ص Suaad	شين ش Sheen
ميم م Meem	لام ل Laam	كاف ك Kaaf	قاف ق Qaaf	فا ف Faa	غين غ Ghaeen
يا ے Yaa	يا ى Yaa	همزة ء Hamzah	ها ه Haa	واو و Wao	نون ن Noon

Lesson No. 2 Combined Letters

Instructions

In this lesson, we'll explore how words are formed by combining letters. We will help students identify and recognize each letter within a word, while also exploring the diverse shapes different letters can take.

ل	لا	با	لا	لا	ا
لك	ک	بلب	لا	ځ	لا
تكث	بكت	كا	كا	كب	كب
با	ى	ن	ث	ت	ب
يس	بس	ثا	با	نا	نا
نخ	تح	ثج	ثس	تس	نس

Lesson No. 2 **Combined Letters**

تم	نم	بم	يم	بج	يح
ثى	تى	نى	يى	بى	ثم
نبن	ثثل	يسل	بيل	تنل	نبل
ح	ج	ثثن	يتن	تين	بنن
يجب	تحت	جت	خب	حث	خ
ته	يه	بة	ه	ة	بخت
د	بهم	بها	يهب	ه	نة

Lesson No. 2 — Combined Letters

جر	ز	ر	خذ	جد	ذ
س	تز	ير	ز	ر	خز
ط	ض	ص	شل	سل	ش
ع	ظا	ضا	طب	صب	ظ
ضغ	صع	غر	عز	ء	غ
ف	ئ	ؤ	أ	تفذ	بعد
قفل	فقل	فو	قو	و	ق

Lesson No. 2 Combined Letters

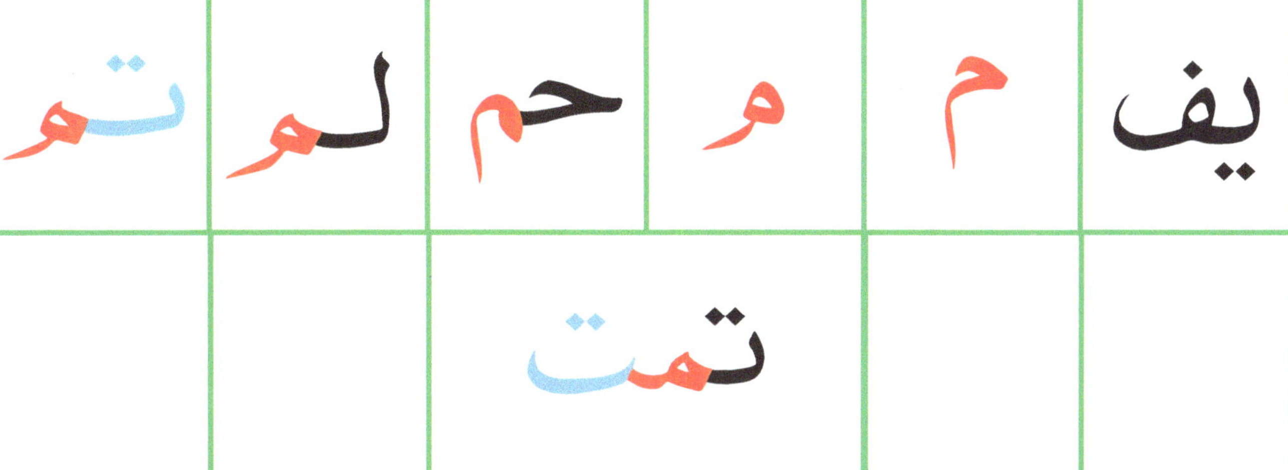

Lesson No. 3 Huroof al Muqatta'at - Disjointed Letters

الٓمٓر	الٓر	الٓمٓصٓ	الٓمٓ
طسٓمٓ	طه	كٓهيعٓصٓ	
حمٓ	صٓ	يسٓ	طسٓ
نٓ	قٓ	عٓسٓقٓ	حمٓ

Lesson No. 4 Harakaat - Movements

Instructions

In Arabic, we have three diacritics called vowel marks that change how we pronounce letters: Fathah (ـَ), Kasrah (ـِ), and Dammah (ـُ). Fathah: Placed above the letter, it gives a short "a" sound (like in "cat"). Kasrah: Placed below the letter, it gives a short "i" sound (like in "hit"). Dammah: Placed above the letter, it gives a short "u" sound (like in "put"). Remember, when reading words with these vowel marks, we don't prolong the sound of the letter. We simply pronounce it clearly and smoothly, without any jerks or pauses.

هُ	هِ	هَ	أُ	إِ	أَ
حُ	حِ	حَ	عُ	عِ	عَ
خُ	خِ	خَ	غُ	غِ	غَ
كُ	كِ	كَ	قُ	قِ	قَ
شُ	شِ	شَ	جُ	جِ	جَ
ضُ	ضِ	ضَ	ىُ	ىِ	ىَ

Lesson No. 4 **Harakaat - Movements**

نُ	نِ	نَ	لُ	لِ	لَ
طُ	طِ	طَ	رُ	رِ	رَ
تُ	تِ	تَ	دُ	دِ	دَ
سُ	سِ	سَ	صُ	صِ	صَ
ظُ	ظِ	ظَ	زُ	زِ	زَ
ثُ	ثِ	ثَ	ذُ	ذِ	ذَ
وُ	وِ	وَ	فُ	فِ	فَ

Lesson No. 4 Harakaat - Movements

Lesson No. 5 The Tanween

Instructions

Double Fathah (ً), Double Kasrah (ٍ) and Double Dammah (ٌ) is called Tanween. Attempt to practise Ikhfa in this lesson. This refers to partially hiding the sound of the letter "Noon" or "Meem" when it comes before certain other consonants. This means pronouncing the "Noon" or "Meem" faintly and connecting it slightly to the next consonant. When Tanween Is followed by a "Throatal letter": Do NOT do Ikhfa. Pronounce the "Noon" or "Meem" clearly without hiding the sound.

بٌ	بٍ	بًا	مٌ	مٍ	مًا
فٌ	فٍ	فًا	وٌ	وٍ	وًا
ذٌ	ذٍ	ذًى	ثٌ	ثٍ	ثًا
زٌ	زٍ	زًا	ظٌ	ظٍ	ظًا

Lesson No. 5 **The Tanween**

صٌ	صٍ	صًا	سٌ	سٍ	سًا
دٌ	دٍ	دًى	ةٌ	تٍ	ةً
رٌ	رٍ	رًا	طٌ	طٍ	طًا
لٌ	لٍ	لًا	نٌ	نٍ	نًا
يٌ	يٍ	يًا	ضٌ	ضٍ	ضًا
جٌ	جٍ	جًا	شٌ	شٍ	شًا
قٌ	قٍ	قًا	كٌ	كٍ	كًا

Lesson No. 5 — The Tanween

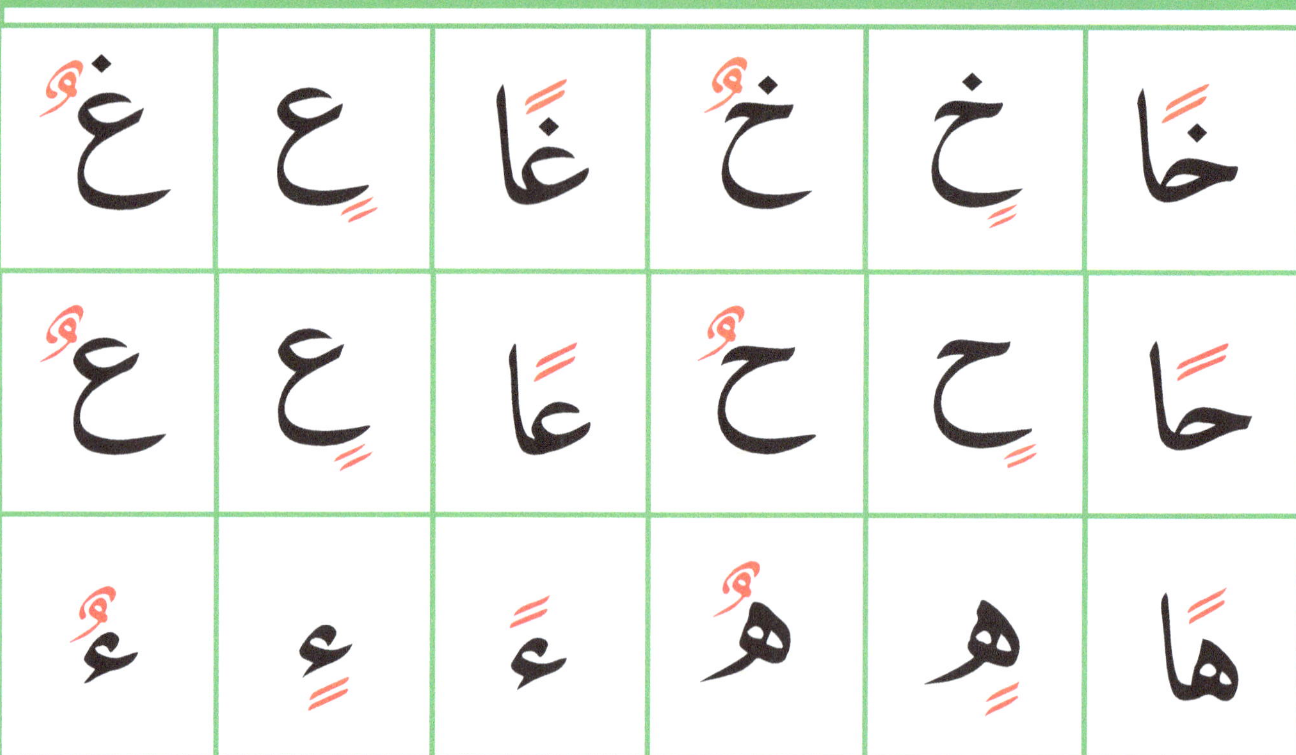

Lesson No. 6 — The Tanween & Movements

Instructions

Students must be able to consistently and accurately connect letters before progressing to ensure fluency in reading aloud. Practice sessions and, if necessary, revisiting the previous lesson, are crucial in mastering this foundational skill.

أَنَاْ	أَمَرَ	أَذِنَ	أَخَذَ	أَحَدٌ	أَبَدًا
حَشَرَ	حَسَدَ	جَمَعَ	جَعَلَ	بَرَرَةٍ	بَخِلَ

Lesson No. 6 The Tanween & Movements

خَشِيَ	خَلَقَ	خُلِقَ	ذَكَرَ	رَفَعَ	رَقَبَةٍ
سُرُرٌ	سَفَرَةٍ	صُحُفًا	وَسَطًا	طَبَقٍ	طَبَقًا
طُوًى	عَبَسَ	عَدَلَ	عَلَقٍ	عَمَدٍ	عِنَبًا
غَبَرَةٌ	فَعَلَ	قَتَرَةٌ	قُتِلَ	قَدَرَ	قُرًى
قَسَمٌ	كَبَدٍ	كُتُبٌ	كَسَبَ	كَفَرَ	كُفُوًا
لُبَدًا	لُمَزَةٍ	لَهَبٍ	مَسَدٍ	نَخِرَةً	وَجَدَ
وَسَقَ	وَقَبَ	وَلَدَ	وَهَبَ	هُمَزَةٍ	هُدًى

Lesson No. 7 Standing Fathah, Kasrah and Dammah

Instructions

Standing Fathah (ٰ), Kasrah (ٖ), and Dammah (ٗ), when elongated, are equivalent in duration to an Alif Maddah (extended Alif). Specifically: Standing Fathah is similar to Alif Maddah in pronunciation. Standing Kasrah is similar to Yā' Maddah (extended Yā').
Standing Dammah is similar to Wāw Maddah (extended Wāw). However, when these elongated vowel marks follow the letters Nūn or Mīm, do not nasalize the Maddah sound. Pronounce it clearly without nasality.

وَٰ	لَٰ	مَٰ	رَٰ	ىَٰ	بَٰ
غَٰ	حَٰ	عَٰ	هَٰ	ءَٰ	نَٰ
ذَٰ	دَٰ	جَٰ	ثَٰ	تَٰ	خَٰ
طَٰ	ضَٰ	صَٰ	شَٰ	سَٰ	زَٰ
هِٖ	إٖ	كَٰ	قَٰ	فَٰ	ظَٰ
ءُٗ		هُٗ		وُٗ	

Lesson No. 8 Madd Wal Leen Alphabets

Instructions

Three letters extend their pronunciation when preceded by specific diacritics: **Alif Maddah:** Pronounced similar to an extended "a" and occurs when an Alif (ا) follows a Fathah (ـَ). **Wāw Maddah:** Pronounced similar to an extended "o" and occurs when a Wāw (و) with a Sukūn (diacritic for no vowel) follows a Dammah (ـُ). **Yā' Maddah:** Pronounced similar to an extended "i" and occurs when a Yā' (ی) with a Sukūn follows a Kasrah (ـِ). These extended sounds are equivalent in duration to one Alif , typically ranging from one to two seconds.

تِی	تُوا	تَا	بِی	بُوا	بَا
حِی	حُوا	حَا	ثِی	ثُوا	ثَا
رِی	رُوا	رَا	خِی	خُوا	خَا
طِی	طُوا	طَا	زِی	زُوا	زَا
فِی	فُوا	فَا	ظِی	ظُوا	ظَا
یِی	یُوا	یَا	هِی	هُوا	هَا

Lesson No. 8 Madd Wal Leen Alphabets

جِى	جُوا	جَا	إِى	أُوا	ءَا
ذِى	ذُوا	ذَا	دِى	دُوا	دَا
شِى	شُوا	شَا	سِى	سُوا	سَا
ضِى	ضُوا	ضَا	صِى	صُوا	صَا
غِى	غُوا	غَا	عِى	عُوا	عَا
كِى	كُوا	كَا	قِى	قُوا	قَا
مِى	مُوا	مَا	لِى	لُوا	لَا

Lesson No. 8 Madd Wal Leen Alphabets

وِى	وُوا	وَا	نِى	نُوا	نَا
دَىْ	دَوْ	ثَىْ	ثَوْ	تَىْ	تَوْ
زَىْ	زَوْ	رَىْ	رَوْ	ذَىْ	ذَوْ
صَىْ	صَوْ	شَىْ	شَوْ	سَىْ	سَوْ
ظَىْ	ظَوْ	طَىْ	طَوْ	ضَىْ	ضَوْ
أَىْ	أَوْ	نَىْ	نَوْ	لَىْ	لَوْ
حَىْ	حَوْ	جَىْ	جَوْ	بَىْ	بَوْ

Lesson No. 8 Madd Wal Leen Alphabets

غَيْ	غَوْ	عَيْ	عَوْ	خَيْ	خَوْ
كَيْ	كَوْ	قَيْ	قَوْ	فَيْ	فَوْ
هَيْ	هَوْ	وَيْ	وَوْ	مَيْ	مَوْ
		يَيْ	يَوْ		

Lesson No. 9 — Exercise of Movement: Standing Fathah, Kasrah and Dammah & Madd Wal Leen & Tanween

Instructions

When the letter "Hamzah" (ء) appears after a "Maddah," the latter takes on different characteristics depending on their relationship:
Maddah Muttasil (جَآءَ): Occurs when Hamzah is within the same word as the Maddah. **Maddah Munfasil** (إِنَّآ أَنْزَلْنَا): Occurs when Hamzah initiates the following word. **Maddah Laazim** (آلْئٰنَ): Occurs when the Maddah is followed by a silent letter (Sukun) within the same word or by specific "Leen" letters. **Maddah Arzi** (جُوعٍ): Occurs when the Maddah is followed by a stop sign (Waqf) at the end of a verse or sentence. All these Madd's are prolonged from three to five seconds.

بِهٖ	أَيْنَ	إِلٰفِ	ءَانِيَةٍ	ءَاوٰى	ءَامَنَ
دَاوٗدُ	خَيْرٌ	خَوْفٍ	جُوعٍ	جِاْىٓءَ	جَآءَ
طَغٰى	شَيْءٍ	مَلِكِ	شَآءَ	رَضُوْا	ذٰلِكَ
فِيهِ	عَيْنٌ	عَلٰى	عَادٍ	طَيْرًا	طَغَوْا
لَوْحٍ	كَيْفَ	كَيْدًا	كَانَ	قَوْلٌ	قَالَ

Lesson No. 9

Exercise of Movement: Standing Fathah, Kasrah and Dammah & Madd Wal Leen & Tanween

لَيۡسَ	مَالًا	نَارًا	مَآءٍ	وَيۡلٌ	يَوۡمٍ
يَرَهٗ	حَاسِدٍ	حَافِظٌ	دَافِقٍ	شَاهِدٍ	عَابِدٌ
عَآئِلًا	غَاسِقٍ	نَاصِرٍ	وَالِدٍ	أَعُوذُ	أَكِيدُ
يَخَافُ	يَدَاهُ	يَقَالُ	تُرَابًا	حِسَابًا	سُبَاتًا
سِرَاجًا	سَلَمٌ	شِدَادًا	شَرَابًا	صَوَابًا	طَعَامٍ
عَذَابٌ	عَطَآءً	عُثَآءً	كِتَابًا	كِرَامًا	لِبَاسًا
لِسَانًا	مَآبًا	مَتَاعًا	مُطَاعٍ	مَعَاشًا	مَفَازًا

Lesson No. 9

Exercise of Movement: Standing Fathah, Kasrah and Dammah & Madd Wal Leen & Tanween

مِهٰدًا	نَبَاتًا	وِفَاقًا	ثُبُوْرًا	رَسُوْلٍ	شُهُوْدٌ
قُعُوْدٌ	وُجُوْهٌ	أَثِيْمٍ	أَلِيْمٍ	بَصِيْرًا	خَبِيْرًا
رَحِيْقٍ	شَهِيْدٌ	عَظِيْمٍ	قَرِيْبًا	كَرِيْمٍ	مَجِيْدٌ
مُحِيْطٌ	نَعِيْمٍ	يَتِيْمًا	يَسِيْرًا	رُوَيْدًا	قُرَيْشٍ
عِيْشَةٍ		اَلْمَوْءُدَةُ		مَوْضُوْعَةٌ	
	مَوٰزِيْنُهٗ		يَوْمَئِذٍ		

Lesson No. 10 — The Sukoon and Jazm

Instructions

Have students memorize the name and shape of jazm and also answer these questions. What is Jazm? What is the letter with a Jazm called? How many times is that letter read or pronounced? Have students distinguish between similarly pronounced letters. Like (ث س ص ذ ز ظ).

أُتْ	إِتْ	أَتْ	أُبْ	إِبْ	أَبْ
أُجْ	إِجْ	أَجْ	أُثْ	إِثْ	أَثْ
أُخْ	إِخْ	أَخْ	أُحْ	إِحْ	أَحْ
أُذْ	إِذْ	أَذْ	أُدْ	إِدْ	أَدْ
أُزْ	إِزْ	أَزْ	أُرْ	إِرْ	أَرْ
أُشْ	إِشْ	أَشْ	أُسْ	إِسْ	أَسْ

Lesson No. 10 The Sukoon and Jazm

أُضْ	إِضْ	أَضْ	أُصْ	إِصْ	أَصْ
أُظْ	إِظْ	أَظْ	أُطْ	إِطْ	أَطْ

Lesson No. 11 The Exercise of Sukoon

Instructions

Q: ***When is Ikhfa done on Noon Sakin and Tanween?***
A: When they are not followed by Throatal Letters.
Q: ***When "Raa" (ر) is Bold?***
A: When the Letter before it is not Yaa Sakin or if the letter before it does not have Kasra.
Q: ***What are bold letters?***
A: (ص ض ط ظ خ غ ق).
Symbols on which to stop: **Waqf-e-Taam (۝), Waqf-e-Lazim (م), Waqf Jaiz (ج), Waqf-e-Mutlaq (ط).**

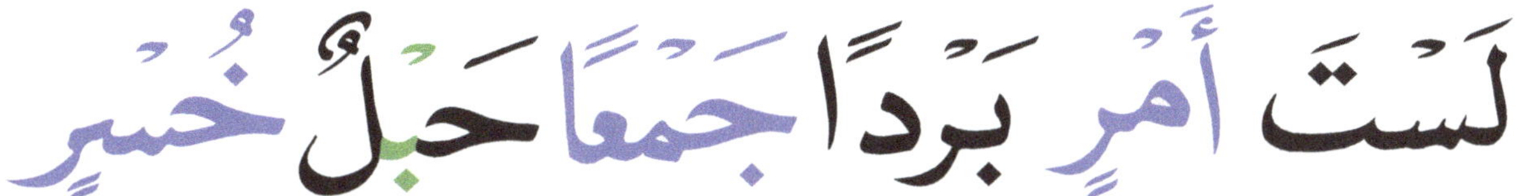

خَلْقًا سَبْحًا سَبْقًا شَأْنُ صُبْحًا ضَبْحًا

Lesson No. 11 The Exercise of Sukoon

عَبْدًا عَدْنٍ عَشْرٍ عَصْفٍ غَرْقًا

غُلْبًا فَصْلُ قَدْحًا قَضْبًا كَأْسًا كَدْحًا

لَغْوًا مِسْكُ نَخْلًا نَشْطًا نَفْسٍ نَقْعًا

يُسْرًا أَبْقَى تَرْضَى تَنْسَى يَخْشَى يَسْعَى

يَتْلُواْ يَدْعُواْ تَجْرِى يَهْدِى يُغْنِى

أَلْقَتْ أَمْهِلْ إِقْرَأْ فَارْغَبْ فَانْصَبْ

وَانْحَرْ أَخْرَجَ أَرْسَلَ أَغْطَشَ أَفْلَحَ

Lesson No. 11 The Exercise of Sukoon

أَكْرَمَ أَلْهَمَ أَنْشَرَ أَنْقَضَ دَمْدَمَ

عَسْعَسَ أَعْبُدُ نَعْبُدُ يَخْرُجُ يَحْسَبُ

يَشْرَبُ يَشْهَدُ تَرْهَقُ تَعْرِفُ أُقْسِمُ

يُبْدِئُ يُنْفَخُ يَنْقَلِبُ يُوَسْوِسُ ثَقُلَتْ

حُشِرَتْ سُطِحَتْ كُشِطَتْ نُشِرَتْ

نُصِبَتْ أَثَرْنَ وَسَطْنَ فَرَغْتَ تَأْتُوْنَ

يُسْقَوْنَ يَفْعَلُوْنَ يَعْمَلُوْنَ يَعْلَمُوْنَ

Lesson No. 11 **The Exercise of Sukoon**

يَضْحَكُونَ يَكْسِبُونَ يَدْخُلُونَ يَنْظُرُونَ

تَعْبُدُونَ أَنْعَمْتَ أَنْذَرْنَا أَنْزَلْنَا خَلَقْنَا

رَفَعْنَا وَضَعْنَا نُطْفَةٍ عِبْرَةٌ زَجْرَةٌ

تَذْكِرَةٌ مُسْفِرَةٌ مُؤْصَدَةٌ مَسْغَبَةٍ

مَقْرَبَةٍ مَتْرَبَةٍ تَضْلِيلٍ تَقْوِيمٍ تَكْذِيبٍ

تَسْنِيمٍ مِسْكِينًا مَمْنُونٍ مَحْفُوظٍ

مَخْتُومٍ مَسْرُورًا مَشْهُودٍ أَبْوَابًا

Lesson No. 11 — The Exercise of Sukoon

مَصْفُوفَةٍ أَزْوَجًا أَشْتَاتًا إِطْعٰمٌ أَعْنَبًا

أَفْوَاجًا أَلْفَافًا قُرْءَانُ ٱلْحَمْدُ وَٱلْفَجْرِ

وَٱلْفَتْحُ وَٱلْعَصْرِ مِنَ ٱلْمُعْصِرٰتِ

مَعَ ٱلْعُسْرِ مَا ٱلْقَارِعَةُ وَ إِذَا ٱلْمَوْءُدَةُ

يَنْظُرُ ٱلْمَرْءُ كَٱلْفَرَاشِ ٱلْمَبْثُوثِ

كَٱلْعِهْنِ ٱلْمَنْفُوشِ لَيْلَةُ ٱلْقَدْرِ

أَخْرَجَتِ ٱلْأَرْضُ مِنْ أَهْلِ ٱلْكِتٰبِ

Lesson No. 11 The Exercise of Sukoon

عِندَ ذِى ٱلْعَرْشِ يَمْنَعُونَ ٱلْمَاعُونَ

وَهُوَ ٱلْغَفُورُ ٱلْوَدُودُ ذُو ٱلْعَرْشِ ٱلْمَجِيدُ

لَقَدْ خَلَقْنَا ٱلْإِنسَـٰنَ فِىٓ أَحْسَنِ تَقْوِيمٍ

أَعْطَيْنَـٰكَ ٱلْكَوْثَرَ ءَآلْـَٔـٰنَ

Lesson No. 12 The Tashdeed

Instructions

Explain the answers to these Questions to your students.

Q: *What is this symbol called (ّ)?*
A: Tashdeed.
Q: *What is the name of Tashdeed Letter?*
A: Mushaddad.
Q: *How many times is the letter with tashdeed recited?*
A: Two Times.
Q: *How is mushaddad recited ?*
A: It is recited with a strong voice.

Lesson No. 12 — The Tashdeed

أُبَّ	أُبّ	أُبُّ	أَبًّا	أَبٍّ	أَبٌّ
إِبًّا	إِبٍّ	إِبٌّ	أُبًّا	أُبٍّ	أُبٌّ
أَتَّ	أَتِّ	أَتُّ	إِتَّ	إِتِّ	إِتُّ
أُتَّ	أُتِّ	أُتُّ	أَتًّا	أَتٍّ	أَتٌّ
إِتًّا	إِتٍّ	إِتٌّ	أُتًّا	أُتٍّ	أُتٌّ
أَثَّ	أَثِّ	أَثُّ	إِثَّ	إِثِّ	إِثُّ
أُثَّ	أُثِّ	أُثُّ	أَثًّا	أَثٍّ	أَثٌّ

Lesson No. 12 The Tashdeed

إِثًّا	إِثٍّ	إِثٌّ	أُثًّا	أُثٍّ	أُثٌّ
أَجَّ	أَجِّ	أَجُّ	إِجَّ	إِجِّ	إِجُّ
أُجَّ	أُجِّ	أُجُّ	أَجًّا	أَجٍّ	أَجٌّ
إِجًّا	إِجٍّ	إِجٌّ			

Lesson No. 13 Exercise of Tashdeed

Instructions

There will always be Ghunna on Meem and Noon Mushaddad.

بُرِّزَ حُصِّلَ صَدَّقَ عَدَّدَ قَدَّرَ

كَذَّبَ نَعَّمَ يَظُنُّ يَحُضُّ جَنَّةٍ ذَرَّةٍ

Lesson No. 13 **Exercise of Tashdeed**

قُوَّةِ كَرَّةُ سُعِّرَتْ قَدَّمَتْ كَذَّبَتْ

زُوِّجَتْ سُجِّرَتْ فُجِّرَتْ سُيِّرَتْ عُطِّلَتْ

كُوِّرَتْ تَطَّلِعُ تُحَدِّثُ نُيَسِّرُ هُمُ ٱلْبَيِّنَةُ

قَيِّمَةُ عَشِيَّةَ مُذَكِّرٌ أَيَّانَ إِيَّاكَ

لِلّٰهِ تَجَلّٰى تَصَدّٰى تَزَكّٰى تَوَلّٰى تَوَّابًا

ثَجَّاجًا غَسَّاقًا فَعَّالٌ كِذَّابًا وَهَّاجًا

مُمَدَّدَةٍ مُكَرَّمَةٍ مُطَهَّرَةٍ وَٱلسَّمَآءِ

Lesson No. 13 — Exercise of Tashdeed

مُمَدَّدَةٍ مُكَرَّمَةٍ مُطَهَّرَةٍ وَالسَّمَآءِ

وَالتَّرَآئِبِ وَالنّٰشِطٰتِ وَالنّٰزِعٰتِ

وَالسّٰبِحٰتِ فَالسّٰبِقٰتِ فَالْمُدَبِّرٰتِ

تُبْلَى السَّرَآئِرُ فَمَهِّلِ الْكٰفِرِيْنَ بِالْخُنَّسِ

الْجَوَارِ الْكُنَّسِ اهْدِنَا الصِّرَاطَ الْمُسْتَقِيْمَ

Lesson No. 14 — Tashdeed with Sukoon

Instructions

If you teach your student this Qaida with all the rules, the students will be able to recite the Holy Qur'an without any difficulty.

مَرُّوْا رَبِّىْ مُدَّتْ حُقَّتْ خَفَّتْ تَبَّتْ

Lesson No. 14 Tashdeed with Sukoon

تَخَلَّتْ قَدَّمَتْ وَٱلصُّبْحِ وَٱلشَّمْسِ

وَٱلشَّفْعِ بِالصَّبْرِ وَٱلصَّيْفِ وَٱلَّيْلِ

وَٱلتِّينِ وَٱلزَّيْتُونِ سِجِّيلٍ سِجِّينٌ

مُنْفَكِّينَ فَإِنَّ ٱلْجَنَّةَ لِحُبِّ ٱلْخَيْرِ

إِذَا ٱلسَّمَآءُ ٱنْشَقَّتْ مَا ٱلطَّارِقُ ٱلنَّجْمُ

ٱلثَّاقِبُ مِنْ شَرِّ ٱلْوَسْوَاسِ ٱلْخَنَّاسِ

Lesson No. 15	Tashdeed with Tashdeed

يَزَّكَّىٰ يَذَّكَّرُ ٱلْمُدَّثِّرُ ٱلْمُزَّمِّلُ

عِلِّيِّينَ عِلِّيُّونَ إِنَّ ٱلَّذِينَ

إِلَّا ٱلَّذِينَ مِنْ شَرِّ ٱلنَّفَّٰثَٰتِ

فَعَّالٌ لِّمَا يُرِيدُ

Lesson No. 16	Tashdeed with Harf Madah

Instructions

Teach students how to connect letters.

ضَآلًّا دَآبَّةٍ حَآجَّكَ حَآجُّوكَ

لَضَآلُّونَ وَلَا ٱلضَّآلِّينَ أَتُحَآجُّونِّ

Lesson No. 16 Tashdeed with Harf Madah

وَلَا تَحَآضُّونَ وَالصَّٰٓفَّٰتِ جَآءَتِ

Lesson No. 17 Ending of Rules

Instructions

If Noon Sakin and Tanween is followed by Yarmaloon Letters: (ی ر م ل و ن) we will do Ghunna with Idgham in all letters except (ر) and (م) where only Idgham will be done. Tell your students not to read the letter before Tashdeed (مَنْ رَبُّكَ), Whenever Noon Sakin and Tanween is followed by (ب) it will be converted into Meem and Ghunna will be done. When Meem Sakin is followed by (ب) or (م) we will do Ghunna on Meem Sakin. If the letter before (ل) in the Word (Allah) has Kasrah (ر) will be light.

إِيَابَهُمْ ۝ خَيْرًا يَرَهُ ۝ شَرًّا يَرَهُ ۝ مِيقَاتًا

يَوْمَ فَمَنْ يَعْمَلْ يَوْمَئِذٍ يَصْدُرُ

Lesson No. 17 Ending of Rules

ٱلنَّاسُ مِن رَّبِّكَ رَسُولٌ مِّنَ ٱللَّهِ

صُحُفًا مُّطَهَّرَةً صَفًّا لَّا يَتَكَلَّمُونَ

قُلُوبٌ يَوْمَئِذٍ وَاجِفَةٌ أَبْصَرُهَا سِرَاجًا

وَهَّاجًا ۝ وَأَنزَلْنَا أَكْلًا لَّمًّا ۝ وَتُحِبُّونَ

ٱلْمَالَ حُبًّا جَمًّا ۝ غُثَآءً أَحْوَىٰ ۝ مُعْتَدٍ

أَثِيمٍ إِذَا تُتْلَىٰ نَارًا حَامِيَةً تُسْقَىٰ مِنْ

عَيْنٍ ءَانِيَةٍ ۝ مَنۢ بَخِلَ لَيُنۢبَذَنَّ

Lesson No. 17 Ending of Rules

مِنۢ بَعۡدِ مِنۢ بَيۡنِ ٱلصُّلۡبِ لَنَسۡفَعًۢا

بِٱلنَّاصِيَةِ بِذَنۢبِهِمۡ مُطَهَّرَةٍۭ بِأَيۡدِي

سَفَرَةٍ كِرَامٍۭ بَرَرَةٍ ۝ هُمۡ فِيهَا لَكُمۡ دِينُكُمۡ

وَلِيَ دِينِ إِنَّ رَبَّهُم بِهِمۡ تَرۡمِيهِم

بِحِجَارَةٍ لَهُم مَّا يَشَآءُونَ مِمَّ ٱللَّهُمَّ

تمّت بِالخَيرِ